CLYDESIDE

THE HERALD
BOOK OF THE CLYDE
VOLUME 3

Clydeside

FACES & PLACES

ROBERT JEFFREY
AND IAN WATSON

BLACK AND WHITE PUBLISHING

First published 2000
by Black & White Publishing Ltd, Edinburgh
ISBN 1 902927 141
Copyright © SMG Newspapers Ltd
Introduction © Robert Jeffrey & Ian Watson

British Library Cataloguing in Publication Data:
A catalogue record for this book is available from the British Library.

Copies of the photographs in this book
are available for personal or commercial use.
Contact: Photo sales department, SMG Newspapers Ltd
200 Renfield Street, Glasgow, G2 3PR,
quoting the page number and a
description of the photograph.

Printed in Spain by Bookprint, S.L.

CONTENTS

ACKNOWLEDGEMENTS

This book is a tribute to the skill and dedication of the
many *Herald* and *Evening Times* staff photographers, whose
work over the decades has produced one of the world's
great picture archives.

The assistance of the following people in
the preparation of this book is gratefully acknowledged:
Samantha Boyd, Rod Ramsay, Rhona Scott and the
staff of the *Herald* and *Evening Times* Picture Library –
Malcolm Beaton, Jim McNeish, Tony Murray, Eva Mutter,
Catherine Turner, Lisa Turner and Grace Gough.

INTRODUCTION

This book is the third in a series of journeys through Scotland's family album, the remarkable picture archive of the *Herald*, *Evening Times* and *Sunday Herald*.

Almost every facet of life in the West of Scotland during the last 100 years is featured among the seven million photographs in this major collection, one of the largest in Europe.

Down the years newspaper photographers have recorded important events in our history, but they have also captured the smaller scale life-enhancing happenings like the annual gala or back court concert. Happenings that collectively create a nostalgic and intriguing picture of the way we were. A constant theme in this look back through the collection is the changing nature of where we live and how we got around.

Many tenements, some worth preserving but others sub-standard slum dwellings, have been bulldozed to be replaced by high rise flats. Hansom cabs gave way to trams (despite fond recollections, the rickety, rattling trams seem to have come off the rails a little too often for comfort!) and eventually the bus and the car took over. The ferries too, a vital method of crossing the winding ribbon of river that splits Glasgow into north and south, are mostly gone, replaced by more prosaic bridges and tunnels.

But not everything changes. These photographs capture the faces of the Clydeside character. Be it a turn-of-century image of children at play or boxers fighting their way out of poverty, or even a shot of the Lord Provost's procession, the faces of Clydeside leap memorably off the page. Ally McLeod, who led the Scotland football team on its infamous foray into the 1978 World Cup Finals in Argentina now commands respect as one our many colourful sporting characters. Apart from Ally others such as Jim Watt and Danny McGrain, heroes whose celebrity extended beyond their sport, are captured at dramatic moments.

The intention is not to present a comprehensive history, a recording of all the tumultuous happenings since the first camera was focused on Clydeside and Clydesiders. Instead the photographs have been chosen to create snapshots of life on the banks of the Clyde down the years.

Browsing through this collection you come across a heart-stopping picture of a fire rescue (that there is no shortage of such photographs testifies to Glasgow's reputation as 'Tinderbox City') or a picture of a little girl drinking from a metal cup chained to a public drinking fountain, a simple image that immediately brings the past back to life.

Or the eye is caught by the curiously named Vinegar Hill, said to commemorate an Irish battle in 1798, underlining a Glasgow penchant for using the names of battlefields such as the equally quirky Schipka Pass near Glasgow Cross. Vinegar Hill became home to the city's annual fair after it was moved from Glasgow Green in 1870 because the council believed it had become 'a vortex of drunken debauchery'. Pictures of this legendary Glasgow institution capture the flavour of the fair, in particular the ever-popular 'cowboy and indian' shows. The growth of holidays 'Doon the Watter' and the rise in popularity of the cinema led to a decline in these spectacular extravaganzas, some of which even featured 'white water' rides on mock rapids!

Despite Glasgow's world-wide reputation for heavy industry there was, surprisingly, a long-lasting rural dimension, even in the heart of the city. How many remember when the east end around Auchenshuggle was open countryside – with a farm called Egypt – or that there was farm in the Gallowgate as late as the thirties? Or fishing boats from Banff moored on the canal in Maryhill? The horse, and with it that gritty character the carter, clad in sack-cloth impervious to all weathers, has all but disappeared from the streets.

All these images are a tribute to the men and women who caught history, as it happened, in their lenses – from the days of plate cameras to the digital devices that in the 21st century transmit directly from laptop computer by mobile phone to join the millions of other pictures in the archive.

We hope that for the reader this new selection from the work of our photographers triggers an evocative journey into our collective memory of the past.

RJ & IW

A **CITY** OF **FACES**

New Year in Glasgow, and indeed all Scotland, has always been a time highly charged with emotion, often fuelled with a dram – or six. The year that has gone looms large in the minds of families, neighbours and friends. The year ahead, as the bells strike out the old, is pregnant with hope.

In Glasgow hundreds made an annual pilgrimage to Glasgow Cross and George Square. In this sea of smiling faces there is little sign of the trying times, the triumphs and tragedies that lie in the uncertain future. This is George Square, Hogmany 1939, on the eve of the Second World War. The Germans were already on the march but in Glasgow it was new year high jinks as usual.

Interestingly, not a bottle or glass in sight. Though it's a safe bet that a drop of the cratur lay hidden in the pockets of the warm woollen raincoats.

'Good luck will rub off when I shake hands with you'. As recently as 1951 the bride still gets a traditional good luck congratulatory kiss from a sweep. Fifty years on with central heating the norm, soot is almost forgotten and white no longer the automatic choice for the bridal gown. Ruby Ford, of Ayr, was a guide mistress who married the local Scoutmaster.

Where did you get those bunnets? These Bridgeton blades were photographed in 1914 by a backcourt photographer. In the sixties Herald columnist William Hunter pondered on the popularity of such huge 'pancakes': did such commodious caps have some other use? The highly respected Elspeth King of the People's Palace in Glasgow Green claims to have heard a rumour that they were handy for catching hot rivets in the yards.

Right: In the background are the Red Road flats built in the mid sixties. They became a famous city landmark at a time when the high rise was a novelty. In contrast to the Bridgeton dandies, these lads are as yet untroubled by fashion as they play on a wrecked car in a makeshift 'adventure playground'.

4

City play again, this time in the Gorbals. Now it's shell suits and trainers. The high rise flats in the background date back to the redevelopment of the sixties. In the last two decades of the twentieth century, housing fashion has swung to the more traditional three or four storey style.

Right: Gorbals street scenes have been irresistible to photographers down the years. This is a classic: kids enjoy themselves in a near-derelict backcourt in the sixties.

Nowadays these youngsters would likely be indoors watching TV. In Glasgow's Grove Street in the early sixties, the playground was the street with the attendant dangers of delivery vans and a broken shop window.

Spot the ball. Further up the river at Blantyre, a rough piece of waste ground is commandeered for a kickabout.

A classic fifties primary school scene. Exercise books open, pencils sharpened at the ready, it's heads down for the boys and girls of class 1B in Glasgow's Hillhead Primary. The pupils' art work is pinned to the painted wood of the walls.

Below: Something of a legend at Glasgow High School, Miss Logan – known to the boys as Miss Nina – leads a group in a bit of choral practice in 1975. The music lesson provided a welcome relief from grammar and sums.

Physical training for the young lads of Allan Glen's, a Glasgow institution with a reputation for training the minds of future scientists and engineers.

Greenock Academy in the fifties, and these girls get instruction on new-fangled electric cookers. On the menu . . . the traditional pancake.

Crossing the road safely was another vital skill to be learned at school. Who can forget the script: look right, look left and look right again – if all clear, cross. This Govan police officer was taking time off from his crime-stopping duties to teach the correct way to cross Elderpark Street in 1952. Parents and passers-by look on approvingly as the smartly dressed youngsters in their warm winter coats get the message.

A rainswept day on Gilmourhill. Freshers' Day – fifties style – at Glasgow University. The formal dress of these new students would soon give way to the hippy gear of the sixties, the loon pants of the seventies and glorious variety of the eighties and nineties.

You didn't need to go to university to get a good education. Many claimed to be honours graduates in 'the college of hard knocks' and picked up much of their knowledge from the hundreds of second-hand book barrows of Clydeside.

This 1915 photograph shows a barrow in the shadow of Paisley Abbey. Earnest would-be buyers cluster round the owner, resplendent in her comfy shawl. During the First World War many a book bought off a barrow was sent to the trenches.

Right: Sometimes an education was the way out of the poverty trap. But for many a youngster the square ring was the route. Fitness and fast fists could earn big money for a fighter with heart. Perhaps the most famous Scot to use this route to wealth was Benny Lynch, a legend whose career ended when he lost his final bout with the bottle.

This, however, is Jim McCann, a fighter who, after his sporting days were over, settled for a steady life as a welder. Here in 1970, at the age of 58, he shows the style he used in the days when he sparred with the immortal Benny.

This eye-catching image was taken in 1985. Boxing booth veterans Fred Tennent (left) and John Kelly had about 40 fights against each other but still managed to remain the best of friends, long after they had taken off the gloves for the last time. Sometimes booth fighters graduated to the halls and the big boxing bills, and the big payouts. Others spent years with the travelling fairs, fighting each other or anyone in the crowd who fancied his chances. The thought that a boxer might make millions fighting a couple of times a year was beyond their dreams. Many survived this hard life, despite battered noses and cauliflower ears, to enjoy a ripe old age.

Jim Watt was a much-loved Glasgow boxer who built up a huge following. His early career was not particularly noteworthy but when he teamed up with Londoner Terry Lawless (left) he won the world title and thrilled Clydesiders with a series of brilliant defences. Here in November 1979 he shows off his WBC belt to the Glasgow Press pack. On retirement Jim, a witty after-dinner speaker, went on to a successful career as a TV boxing pundit.

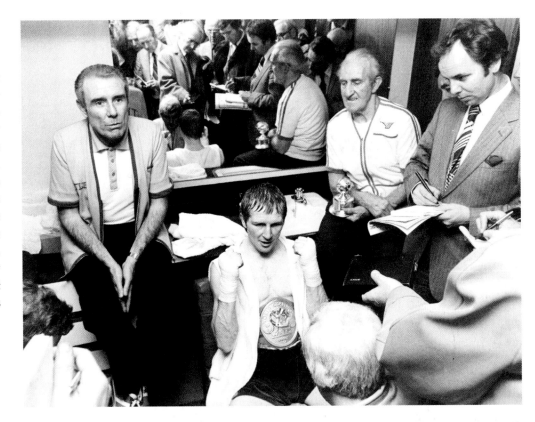

Peter Keenan, the legendary PK, was a huge favourite of Clydeside fight fans. He filled halls and football stadiums alike when at his peak. Here he shows off one of his two Lonsdale Belts with trainer Alec Adams on his right and manager Tommy Gilmour on his left. Peter, who never won a world title, was however the only Scot to win two Lonsdale Belts. On retirement from the ring he became a boxing promoter and for a time ran a pub on the banks of the Clyde at Anderston Quay. A real Glaswegian character held in great affection in the city, he sadly died in July 2000.

Icelander Thorloff Beck of St Mirren leaves Rangers stars Jim Baxter and Eric Caldow in his wake as he bears down on goal. Foreign players dominate the game in Britain these days but in the sixties Scandinavians were amongst the first to add an international flavour to the Scottish game. Later Beck made the short trip from Paisley to Govan to don the light blue of Rangers.

Left: Danny McGrain's smile to the camera says it all as Celtic beat arch rivals Rangers to lift the 1980 Scottish Cup. The great Davie Cooper, who died at the tragically young age of 39 in March 1995, is the dejected Rangers player. Later a pitched battle between rival supporters marred the celebrations.

The Tartan Army follows Scotland around the world. Their 'Que Sera Sera' attitude make them welcome from Buenos Aires to Belgrade despite their team's minimal impact on world football. These 1987 footsoldiers were in jovial mood for the visit of England to Hampden. The Braveheart style of face painting was in an early stage of development.

Scott's porridge oats, Cadbury Flakes and Heinz 57 varieties – not quite a continental deli-
catessen, but this picture captures the essence of the Barras, the world-famous street market just
a few hundred yards from Glasgow Cross.

There was a great deal of work to be done in the heyday of the Clyde, dredging the channel and diving to keep dock gates and equipment up to scratch. Here in the sixties, Clyde Port Authority diver David Bell G.M. gets down to the task of scrubbing his rubber suit and heavy brass helmet.

Right: Long queues on the pavement in all weathers for a seat in the cinema are no longer as commonplace as in the fifties, when buskers earned a bob or two keeping the punters entertained before they were entertained!

Christmas dinner 1950 at Erskine Hospital for war veterans. Still mired in post-war austerity, Britain was a long way from today's affluent wine drinking society. These old soldiers, complete with medals, share a bottle of beer.

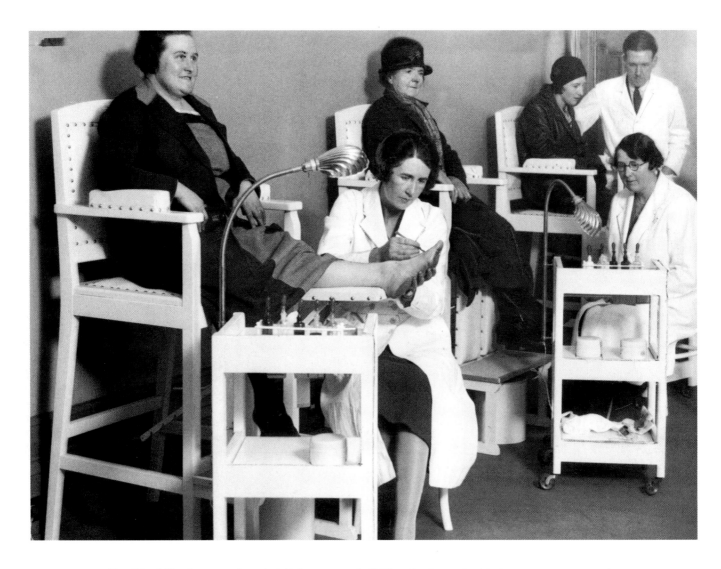

The Herald's photographers left little unrecorded! Here in the early thirties some matrons take the weight of their feet while the white-coated technicians of the Glasgow Foot Hospital in Windsor Terrace get down to work. The hats add a strange formality to the proceedings.

Glasgow still gets the occasional heatwave though memory seems to suggest they were more frequent in the past. George Square is, however, still the place to be when the summer sun shines down. These late-forties office girls put their post-war worries aside to make the most of the weather.

Left: In today's health-conscious society, drinking from a communal cup would be frowned upon. In the fifties though, this was the way to slake a thirst during a long hot day in the park.

Glasgow's Lord Provost's procession in June is always a big attraction. Susan Baird, a popular Lord Provost in the late eighties and early nineties, has a smile almost as wide as her chain of office as her coach leads the parade through the streets.

COBBLES, CAURS
AND CRANES

Rush hour 1914 style. Trams, horse-drawn carts and pedestrians converge on Glasgow Bridge at the foot of Jamaica Street at 5pm on a March evening.

The old Glasgow Bridge – later it became known as the Jamaica Bridge – in 1895, this time looking north from the south bank towards the famous landmark of Paisley's the outfitters, now gone.

Fog was a menace on Clydeside until the clean air acts of the fifties. Smoke from domestic fires mixed with the naturally occurring mists of the west coast to produce scenes of spectacular gloom. This photograph was taken in Union Street in 1948. Some older folk would say this was almost a clear day – you could at least see the trams instead of feeling your way home along the tram rails in the middle of the road.

St Enoch Station, here in its full turn of the century magnificence, was the departure point for many of the trains to the coast. The station closed in 1966 but the hotel, a favourite venue for glittering events, remained open until 1974. Its Victorian marble and mahogany was replaced by the glass shopping palace of the modern St. Enoch Centre.

The 'Hielanman's Umbrella' in Argyle Street in the late fifties. The railway bridge out of Central Station – historically a meeting place for highlanders in Glasgow – may have kept the rain off these commuters but you can almost feel the chill of the November night air.

A wet December night looking down the Renfield Street from St. Vincent Street, with the much-loved Barr's Irn Bru neon advertisement glowing cheerfully through the drizzle.

This 1927 motorist on the Duntocher to Anniesland boulevard had to turn back at Blairdardie as the bridge over the Forth and Clyde Canal had yet to be built. The delay in completing the bridge had arisen because negotiations between Glasgow Corporation and London Midland and Scottish Railways, who were responsible for the canal, had become somewhat protracted. The fields in the background would become the garden suburb of Knightswood within the next ten years.

As in many of the world's great cities, a river creates a dramatic North/South divide that requires crossing points galore – tunnels, ferries and bridges. In the case of the Clyde, both elegant and functional. This aerial view also takes in the High Court and the St Enoch Centre on the banks of an unusually still river.

Right: It is only a little more than forty years since this photograph was taken, but the area is almost unrecognisable from the way it looks today. Fairfield's Govan yard is in the foreground, ships are on the stocks in various stages of construction. Others lie moored at the dockside and cranes galore line the river banks. A small ferry is caught in mid-crossing and dredgers are ready to continue the endless work of keeping the channel deep enough for the seaborne traffic of the fifties. The smog of industry drifts across the north bank towards the post-war housing scheme of Drumchapel.

Scotland's first purpose-built mosque seen here under construction. It was completed in 1985 and replaced a temporary building in the Gorbals which had been established in the forties.

Left: Winter sunshine on the suspension bridge linking Carlton Place and Clyde Street. Just beyond the silhouette of the Sheriff Court is the minaret of Glasgow's Islamic Centre and Mosque.

January 1950 and an electric milk float and a sturdy carthorse both have to cope with abominable conditions underfoot while a coating of snow adds to the nobility of George Square's many statues.

Left: The Clyde Tunnel and the Kingston and Erskine Bridges killed off the Renfrew and Erskine ferries as vehicle carriers across the river, although the Renfrew ferry remains in a pedestrian-only version. This was the Erskine Ferry on a quiet day. Often queues of cars backed up from both banks.

This is Langside Drive in Glasgow's south side caught in the grip of typical January snowfall in 1987. Note that Clydeside trait of total disregard of the danger of taking to the road rather than the footpath.

The old and new Gorbals dramatically juxtaposed in 1962. The tower blocks rise under the tall cranes while the empty fireplaces of the old tenements are a bleak reminder of homes where generations grew up in difficult and overcrowded conditions.

Few would mourn the loss of slum tenements but Glasgow lost many fine buildings to make way for the M8 motorway. The Grand Hotel at Charing Cross bites the dust in March 1969.

Left: The community spirit of tenement life is fondly remembered by many who moved to the peripheral schemes but this picture is a stark reminder that the reality was often a squalid slum.

Chipmunks of the Glasgow University Air Squadron on a training flight over the University and Kelvingrove Art Gallery and Museum in 1953.

Right: Pomp and ceremony at Glasgow Cathedral in April 1956. The occasion was a visit by the Duke of Gloucester, Colonel of the Scots Guards, to unveil a stained glass window in honour of the regiment.

Charles Rennie Mackintosh's work attracts tourists galore to visit the House for an Art Lover in Bellahouston Park, Scotland Street School and Hill House in Helensburgh as well as his masterpiece, the Glasgow School of Art. This night shot of the school dramatically highlights its innovative design.

Right: A classic fifties scene looking west along Sauchiehall Street to Charing Cross. In the distance is the Grand Hotel, demolished in 1969 to make way for the motorway. In the foreground is the striking art deco style Beresford Hotel which later became student accommodation.

Glasgow's George Square is a focal point for exhibitions, concerts and demonstrations of all kinds. This memorable image shows the depth of feeling against nuclear weapons as the square is littered with symbolic dead in 1983.

George Square again, this time during the Second World War. How the giant Lancaster bomber P for Peter made it into the Square to feature in a Wings for Victory fund raising was never made clear.

Right: Despite the explosion of designer shops in Glasgow, the lure of Paddy's Market – just off the Clyde in behind the High Court – remains strong for those more concerned with price than label.

Glaswegians would barely recognise the Duke of Wellington without a traffic cone for a hat. The statue outside the Gallery of Modern Art, formerly Stirling's Library, in Royal Exchange Square has long been a lure for revellers showing their agility after a pint or two, especially at weekends.

HEADLINES AND DEADLINES

Turnberry Hotel over-looking the Firth of Clyde near Girvan is a legendary destination for luxury golfing holidays, famed round the world. The grounds look somewhat different in 1917 when the officers and men of the Aerial Gunnery School posed for the camera.

Right: Still on a military theme, Earl Haig, the controversial World War One general, inspects the Guard of Honour at the unveiling of the Cenotaph in Glasgow in 1924.

Another ceremonial occasion, this time in 1928 as King George V opens the Glasgow bridge named in his honour. Along with the King and Queen Mary is Lord Provost David Mason and Mrs Mason. We can only speculate on the identify of the gent standing in the background.

Below: This is the Order of St John of Jerusalem procession en route from Glasgow Cathedral to Provand's Lordship in 1950. Tram rails and cobbles are a hazard and the Food Control Sub Office appears to be a hangover from the war.

Right: Local dignitaries address a gathering from the Mercat Cross at Glasgow Cross.

Duke Street Prison, or jail as it was known to Glasgow eastenders, was demolished to make way for housing in the late fifties. The trap door in the execution chamber held a macabre fascination for this group of reporters being shown around.

A huge crowd gathers for a launch at John Brown's shipyard in Clydebank in the twenties. Today's commuters will envy the three shilling (15p) weekly return to Glasgow!

The Glen Cinema disaster is Britain's forgotten tragedy. Seventy Paisley children were suffocated, crushed or trampled to death behind the locked emergency door on Hogmanay 1929. This was the scene outside the cinema on New Year's Day 1930. Ironically a film called *The Crowd* is advertised. The day before about 1000 children were packed in to watch *The Desperate Dude* when a reel of film caught fire creating smoke and panic which led to the appalling loss of life. The tragedy was responsible for the introduction of new laws on cinema safety.

During the first week of January 1930 Paisley's Streets were filled with a seemingly endless procession of small coffins. Here the lines of graves in Hawkhead cemetery make a heart-rending scene.

The crowds both in the cemeteries and the streets emphasise the shock of the loss of so many young Paisley lives. One family lost three children, three families two each. As the whole town mourned, donations and messages of sympathy flooded in from around the globe.

Right: You can almost hear the rattle of the wheels on the cobbles in this evocative picture in St Enoch Square of Glasgow's last horse-drawn cab in 1931. Wrapped against the weather, his cab shining and his topper polished, the cabbie drives through streets now filled with petrol-driven cars, lorries and buses.

The Glasgow motor show, held in the Kelvin Hall until the advent of the Scottish Exhibition Centre, has always been a popular event. In 1935 the big attraction was Sir Malcolm Campbell's land speed record-breaking 'Bluebird' whose sleek lines contrast with the more conventional cars on show.

In 1938 Glasgow staged the memorable Empire Exhibition in Bellahouston Park. A wet summer was blamed for the exhibition's failure to make its target of twenty million. 'Only' twelve and a half million turned out to savour its delights. The striking Tait's tower, named after the architect, was demolished despite widespread protest. It could have been Glasgow's Eiffel Tower.

Censorship meant that the original Second World War caption described this scene as 'rescue party at work on a damaged tenement in a West of Scotland town' and the picture was passed for publication. The actual scene of destruction was Greenock.

Another picture passed by the censor – a now world-famous image of Radnor Street, Clydebank in March 1941. The archive caption notes that the photograph was passed for publication by the General Section of the Ministry of Information on 11 September 1944.

The Erskine Ferry lies in the icy Clyde against a backdrop of Old Kilpatrick and the snow-covered Kilpatrick Hills. This photograph was also censored, eventually being released for publication in 1945.

Left top: A rare shot of the inside of Maryhill Barracks where many a raw recruit was introduced to army life. The last soldiers left in 1958 and the barracks were demolished to make way for the Wyndford housing scheme. Remnants of the barrack walls can still be seen today.

Left bottom: April 1940 and this parade of troops was part of a fund raising flag day on behalf of the Glasgow Central War Relief Fund. Here they march outside Glasgow City Chambers. The legendary Lord Provost Paddy Dollan took the salute.

Generally speaking, Glasgow's trams were a safe means of transport but accidents did happen and this one looks serious: the caption tells us only that many were injured. The impressive spread of billboards is evocative of the time, probably 1939 when 'Gunga Din', and 'In Name Only', both starring Cary Grant, were on release, and Rob Wilton was on the bill at the Empire.

Rare occurrences or not, a photographer was usually around to capture the scene when a tram left the rails. Twenty people were injured in this collision involving a tram and a lorry at the junction of Jamaica Street and Broomielaw in June 1954. A police mountie keeps an eye on the crowd as an ambulance stands by.

You wait half an hour for a bus . . . then one comes through your front window! This unfortunate woman surveys the wreckage in the bay window of her Langlands Road home in January 1953.

Less dramatic than a bus coming through your window, but no doubt the passengers in this Springburn tram had a heart-stopping moment when it was pushed into the pavement in a collision. The accident happened in Govan Road, Linthouse in 1954.

Work proceeds in a seemingly unhurried but chaotic fashion on a traffic alteration at Eglinton Toll in August 1946. The pub in the picture – McNees – was a popular south side howff, just yards from the famous Plaza dance hall.

Jamaica Street, September 4, 1962 – the day of the last parade of trams through the city. Heavy rain failed to stop the party and thousands lined the streets to say their farewell to a much-loved mode of transport. Youngsters grasped the last chance to place a penny on the rails and have it bent by the tram wheels.

Left: Many Glasgow tenements had poor or non-existent foundations and building collapses were not infrequent. This one at Balmano Brae in 1951 left several families homeless.

If tenements didn't always collapse they had on occasion to be evacuated if they became dangerous. In the top left of this shot a Mr McGrattan leans out his top flat window, refusing to leave the endangered building at 148 Salamanca Street in Glasgow. Policemen were posted at the close to keep out anyone with a similar reluctance to give up their home.

Glasgow acquired a perhaps deserved but unwanted reputation as 'tinder box city'. Fires frequently brought the city centre to a standstill as on this night in February 1971 when Wypers restaurant in Renfield Street went up in flames.

Left: A dramatic shot catches workers in statuesque poses as they demolish the Arnott Simpson department store after it was destroyed by a fire in 1951.

The St Andrew's Halls, behind the Mitchell Library at Charing Cross, was a much-loved venue for classical and jazz concerts. Some of music's greatest names appeared here and there was genuine shock in the city when the famous building was destroyed by fire in October 1962. Firemen fought a long and spectacular, but ultimately futile, battle to save the landmark.

The dramatic rescue of a shop assistant from the tragic fire at Grafton's gown shop in Argyle Street in 1949. Thirteen shop assistants lost their lives and Mr Soloman Winetrobe was awarded the George medal for saving five women.

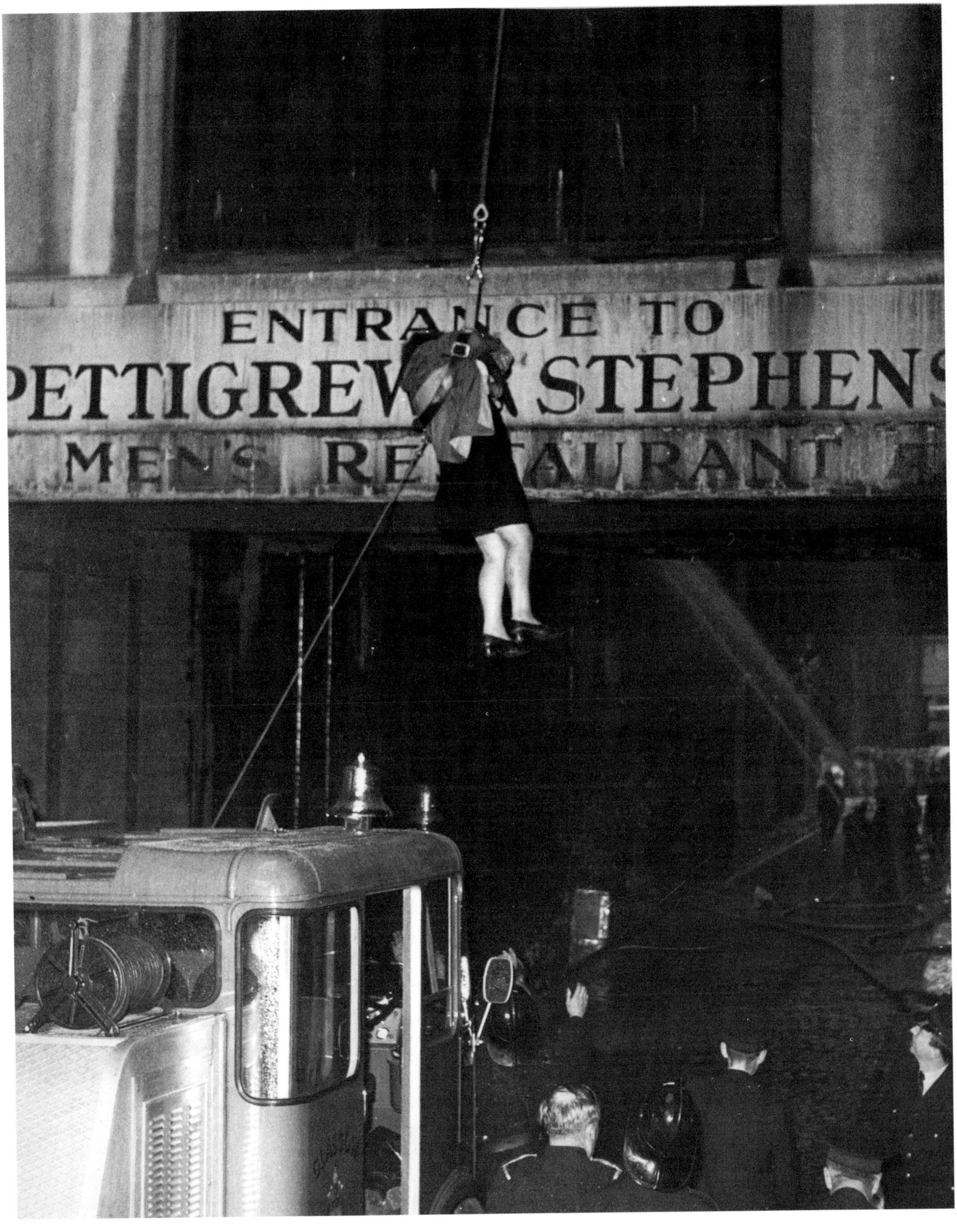
ENTRANCE TO
PETTIGREW STEPHENS
MEN'S RESTAURANT

The Cheapside Street fire in 1960 is etched in the Clydeside memory. Nineteen firemen lost their lives tackling the blaze at a whisky warehouse. This poignant photograph shows the crowds in silent tribute as the funeral procession makes its way along the High Street to Glasgow Cathedral.

Left: Another shop fire, this time Pettigrew and Stephens department store in Sauchiehall Street. The fire service was quickly on the scene to rescue this woman employee.

In the twenties many families headed across the Atlantic for a new life. Optimism radiates from the faces of this family of ten from Dumbarton as, under the watchful eye of an officer, they line up for the camera before boarding a Canadian Pacific Railways liner. Did they find happiness?

Some left for greener, cleaner pastures but some remained and got stuck into environmental improvements projects! Toddler Ian Francis is seen here doing his bit to clean up the Forth and Clyde Canal at Maryhill in 1974.

The car manufacturing industry returned to Scotland in the early sixties when government's regional policy persuaded the Rootes group set up in Linwood near Paisley. This is May 3, 1963 and the Duke of Edinburgh drives a Hillman Imp after formally opening the plant. In the passenger seat is Lord Rootes.

A life in politics has its highs and lows. Teddy Taylor, once a young Conservative councillor in the old Glasgow Corporation and later popular MP for Cathcart, suffered a knock in 1979 with a dramatic General Election defeat at the hands of John Maxton of the famous political dynasty. Teddy went south and was soon back in the Commons. But there is no hiding his sadness and that of his wife Sheila in the aftermath of a defeat which was all the more painful for a Tory in the face of a famous political victory for Mrs Thatcher.

Left: After a troubled history the Linwood plant finally closed in 1981. This 1980 photograph of stockpiled cars suggests the vehicles may have moved more speedily out of the factories than the showrooms.

Another young political prodigy in action – this time Brian Wilson at a Campaign for Nuclear Disarmament meeting near Dunoon in 1977. Brian went on to feature prominently in Scottish political life and became a government minister after Tony Blair's landslide victory for New Labour in 1997.

Right: The south bank of the Clyde sprang to life in the summer of 1988 when Glasgow hosted the Garden Festival, a government-backed urban regeneration initiative. Few of the landmarks in the photograph remain in 2000. The site, Pacific Quay, is undergoing a radical transformation into a Science Centre which includes 3D cinemas, a 400ft tower as well as interactive displays.

Argentina '78! What Scottish football fan can forget the nightmare of overweaning optimism followed by abject defeat. Manager Ally McLeod names his World Cup squad to the waiting Press pack led by the legendary Jimmy Sanderson in his trademark pinstripe suit. Ally survived his fall from grace in South America and is fondly remembered as one of the game's great characters.

Right: Another scene that football fans of a certain vintage will not forget: piles of beer cans at the end of the match, this one at Hampden Park in the sixties. When the Criminal Justice Act outlawed alcohol from sports grounds in the early eighties, scenes like this became a distant memory.

A dramatic picture of mounted police breaking up the pitched battle between rival fans at the end of the Rangers v Celtic Scottish Cup Final at Hampden in May 1980. The ugly scenes, which went round the world on television, tarnishing Glasgow's reputation, led to the legislation that banned booze inside grounds.

4

LAUNCHES AND LEGENDS

Clyde launches were mostly routine affairs. So many ships came off the stocks in the heyday of shipbuilding that the yard workers were well used to launching lengthy ships into a narrow river. But on this occasion in 1954 *HMS Keppel*, built at Yarrows, caused a minor incident by brushing the scaffolding of another ship under construction.

Left: The *Queen Elizabeth 2* needs a helping hand as she inches her way into Greenock Dry Dock in 1968.

Right: Something of a nautical traffic jam as the *Uganda,* under tow, passes the *Waverley* near the Erskine Bridge. The liner served as a school ship and is well remembered by the thousands of pupils who sailed in her.

Below: If launching into the narrow Clyde was a skilful exercise, the even narrower Cart could be just as tricky. This Paisley launch took place in midwinter with the fields thick with snow. Apt, as the vessel concerned was a cargo/passenger steamer strengthened specially as an ice breaker. The *Cabot Strait* took to the water in 1947.

In the forties the Clyde was an important artery for trade. This puffer, the *Faithful*, laden with a cargo of sand, found that low water was just too low and ran aground at Jamaica Bridge.

Fishing boats from the highlands and islands crowd the famous Bergius Yard at Dobbie's Loan in the heart of Glasgow on the Forth and Clyde Canal. They were in town to be fitted with Kelvin diesel engines.

The *Sunset* pulls up her nets off Largs in the Clyde Estuary, some way from her home port of Cullen in the north east of Scotland.

The Finnieston Ferry crosses to the south side of the river under an ominous sky. The cranes on General Terminus Quay were a Glasgow landmark until they were blown up by demolition squads in 1981.

The ferry crossing at Govan was an important link between north and south banks, particularly for shipyard workers. In the background the vehicular ferry brings over a load of lorries while the passenger ferry seems to be having a quiet time in this 1957 picture.

The grim reality of post-war life in the late forties is caught in this evocative photograph. In the foreground a packed passenger ferry heads for the north bank.

The tug played a vital role in the days when the river was busy with commercial traffic as well as the comings and goings from the yards. Here they control the *Circassia*, despite the difficulty of wind and current, on the way to her berth at Yorkhill Quay in Spring 1958.

Once a famous landmark in the city centre, RNVR *Carrick* now languishes in a derelict state at Irvine, hoping that money can be found for restoration. Here she is seen in 1949 making her way up river to her Clyde Street mooring as HQ of the Royal Navy Volunteer Reserve Club.

Right: Older Glaswegians will remember the 'shipwreck' in Clyde Street in 1978. At a particularly low tide *The Carrick* took the bottom, then, caught against the quayside as the tide rose, she canted heavily over to starboard and flooded, causing a great deal of damage. Refloated and refurbished, she resumed her role as HQ of the RNVR until, sadly, she took the bottom once again in July 1989, flooded, and this time was written off as a constructive total loss. She was acquired by the Clyde Ship Trust for renovation and moved to the Maritime Museum at Irvine in 1992. Originally she was known as the 'City of Adelaide' and the folk there have begun raising money to save the vessel.

105

Tall ships *L'Avenir* and *Ponape* make a fine picture as their elegant masts tower from Prince's Dock in 1934 when sailing ships still played an important commercial role.

A particularly fine shot of the sail training vessel *Sir Malcolm Miller* as she approaches Greenock in 1987. The spars and rigging have a full compliment of crew members making for a spectacular sight as the ship enters port.

Under the command of Sir Francis Drake the original *Golden Hind* sailed the oceans of the world. This replica vessel is seen here in the Firth of Clyde while on an adventurous expedition round Britain in the early nineties.

The *Queen Mary* was a favourite for trips 'Doon the Watter'. Shortly after leaving service she was captured here 'pushing up the daisies' in Lamont's Yard in Greenock. The steamer, which for a time changed her name to *Queen Mary II* in deference to the legendary Cunarder, is now a pub/restaurant in the heart of London, moored near Waterloo Bridge. A somewhat sad end.

Grime-caked after war service as a troop ship, the *Empress of Scotland* is towed into Fairfield's basin in 1948 for a facelift before returning to the glamorous life of a passenger liner.

Another Cunarder makes its way down to sea from John Brown's shipyard. No big crowds this time, just a family group waving as the *Carinthia* passes Erskine in 1956.

Coastal waters can be hazardous and even the most experienced skipper can come to grief. Two tugs tow the *Montclair* off the rocks at the Isle of Cumbrae in 1931.

'In her white beauty she lies – a swan among the ducklings of commerce' waxed the original caption for the 1931 picture of the graceful steam yacht *Eileen* which was built at John Brown's. She is seen here berthed on the Clyde near the mouth of the River Kelvin.

Left: Fairfield's shipyard, January 1955, and work progress on the *Empress of Britain*, somewhat rough and ready scaffolding hiding her elegance and beauty.

A well earned cuppa from the ubiquitous tea can for these 1967 shipyard workers. The *QE2* takes shape in the background.

As sunset silhouettes the shipyard cranes, a tug ploughs its way upstream at Meadowside. The evocative picture captures the industrial character of the river.

Workers clamber over piles of drag chain in preparations for the launch of the *Uganda* in January 1952. These working conditions and clothing – not a hard hat in sight – fall well short of modern health and safety standards. The yards were dangerous, dirty places in which to create complex and beautiful ships.

WORKING FOR A LIVING

In the heart of Lowther Hills, near the headwaters of the Clyde, is the lead mining village of Wanlockhead. The mine is long closed but this picture from 1953 captures the bleakness of the mine head.

In this atmospheric image of Motherwell on a cold January day in 1954, the steelworks belch smoke in the background beyond the railway sidings and Fyffes banana warehouse.

A dramatic sky over Ravenscraig, a potent symbol of post war industrial Scotland. The furnaces in the Lanarkshire steelworks went cold in 1992 with the loss of around 4000 jobs at the former British steel plant which had begun life in 1957 owned by the Colvilles iron and steel company.

The Clydebridge steel works was an older Colvilles plant. This 1939 photograph was taken in tribute to a new record weekly production of more than 7000 tons of steel plates – all no doubt of great value to the war effort. The foreman, like his contemporaries in the shipyard, marks his status with a bowler as he records the glowing metal rolling of the presses.

Left: Back to Ravenscraig, this time the melting shop in 1963. You can almost feel the heat as the molten steel is poured from ladle into mould. Dangerous work in difficult conditions.

Glasgow Corporation Cleansing Department at one time had the biggest stable of Clydesdale horses in Britain – 370. But by the fifties, when these pictures were taken, the advent of the internal combustion engine had reduced the numbers to forty. Here four of these beautiful animals are fed in the Kilbirnie Street HQ.

A cleansing worker and his Clydesdale begin a day's work. The public had great affection for these gentle giants of workhorses. In their final years the department put them onto nightshift and in by 1956 motor-powered dust carts had taken over. Progress?

Back in 1942, Mr Pete Ballingall is the man in charge of this cleansing department horse and cart. Today's outfit for a cleansing worker is somewhat different from Mr Ballingall's three-piece suit and bunnet.

Horse-drawn carts were, surprisingly, still very much in evidence in the early sixties, especially at the fruit market in Candleriggs. The cart loaded with potatoes in the foreground relies on shanks' pony though.

This farmyard scene was taken in Soho Street, near Gallowgate in the thirties. Not the ideal home for sheep, donkey or geese! Surprisingly one or two farmsteads survived close to the centre of the city long after the fields gave way to tenements. One famous farm in Tollcross was called Eygpt – simply because the owner had served there in the Army.

Not a kiwi fruit or an avocado in sight in the fruit market in the sixties. A worker takes his not inconsiderable weight off his feet, surrounded by cabbage and turnips. Fruit market workers were famous for their disregard of the weather, working without protective clothing whatever the season.

The merchants cast their expert eyes over the goods and men in bunnets discuss the comings and goings in this 1930s fruit market scene.

In the days before the factory acts carried much bite, work could be hot and sweaty. Elizabeth Douglas and Christine O'Connor found some relief from the heat and humidity by going barefoot when spinning cotton in the Greenock Ropeworks mills at New Lanark.

Walker's sugar factory was a major employer in Greenock in the fifties. These factory girls are packing caster sugar in one pound bags, perhaps dreaming of the rock and roll heroes of the era such as Elvis and Bill Haley?

February 1954 and this group of Paisley mill workers seem in good spirits as they leave after a hard shift at Ferguslie Mills.

Templeton's carpet factory in Bridgeton in the late thirties and these workers are giving the final product a brush up before despatch. The famous factory had a tragic side to its history with a wall collapse in 1889 killing thirty workers while a fire in 1900 killed another seventy people. Nonetheless the firm went on to produce carpets of world renown.

Being in hospital was no fun at any time, but Christmas could be especially hard. These nurses at the Royal Hospital for Sick Children in 1934, however, are doing a wonderful job in making sure their young patients don't miss out on the fun and the presents.

Not exactly a glamorous scene, this was the 'steamie' in Rutherglen Road in the early eighties. These public wash houses played an important role in city life before the kitchen washing machine took over. They also doubled as social centres and the humour and sometimes the pathos of the steamie were brilliantly caught in Tony Roper's famous play of that name.

Right: A woman in a man's world: Mrs Mary Scott looks well able to hold her own in the tough environment of the shipyards in the fifties. She is the rivet catcher. The 'rivet heater' throws the rivet from the furnace to be caught in the catcher's tongs.

The mass meeting was a vital part of shipyard life. Many a politician, comedian and journalist learned their skills as a convener of shop stewards. Here Mr Alex Jamieson explains a point to a meeting of workers at Fairfields in 1965.

In the fifties, so many women were recruited as tram drivers that they had their own caur driving school. Here a woman trainee driver gets instruction in Copelaw Street. The tram clippie with the time-honoured phrase, 'C'MOAN GET AFF' is well remembered, but up front many women drove the tram.

PLAYING FOR REAL

Fairgrounds don't seem to have lost their magic even today. This fascinating picture was taken around 1915 of a ride called the High Flyer, a major attraction at Vinegar Hill, a showground at Camlachie in Glasgow's east end. Vinegar Hill is said to be named in commemoration of a battle in Ireland.

Wild west shows were a big attraction at the fairs of the late 19th and early 20th centuries. This photograph from Vinegar Hill around 1915 shows the baddie making his getaway, although the girls on the right don't seem too worried!

The sight of horse-drawn caravans parked in the show people's camp site makes a bleak contrast to the excitement and fun of the fair.

Even in the rain the fairground was a magnet for families in search of a fun day out. This is Vinegar Hill during the First World War.

Penguins have an irresistible magic. This toddler, let off his reigns for a moment, offers to share his crisps. The lad in the background is keeping his gobstopper firmly where it belongs. Calderpark Zoo, 1958.

Left: New Lanark, a visionary industrial experiment, is now visited by tourists from around the world who enjoy the restored mills which recall the socialist concept of Robert Owen. Fairs and car rallies to the village add to the fun. Here young Kenneth Middleditch looks the part driving his father's miniature steam tractor at a Victorian Day.

'Come in number eight, your time's up'. Rouken Glen, Easter Monday 1957, and these two lads in a 'catacanoe' are having some difficulty avoiding a collision. One of them uses his oar to fend off the larger boat.

Members of Glasgow Steamer Society used Rouken Glen Pond on the south side in the sixties to enjoy sailing their models. No doubt the hobby of building model ships was a by-product of living in Clydeside and daily contact with the real thing. This comprehensive group has a real Clyde feel to it – paddlers, a Sealink ferry and a Firth of Clyde pleasure vessel.

For youngsters there is no such thing as the wrong type of snow. This 'choo-choo' train of sledges took to the slopes of Burnside in 1949. The trusty hound shares in the enjoyment in a scene replicated in every Clydeside park whenever there is a decent snowfall.

Right: Queen's Park recreation ground in the forties. Modest slope for the sledges but the amateur footballers don't let the winter gloom or the icy surface spoil the fun. And a fair-sized crowd are keen enough to stand on frosty touchlines on a bitterly cold Saturday afternoon. No doubt some would enjoy a warming cup of tea from the residents of the post war prefabs in the background.

Gee up! The kilted young man will have to wait for the next turn as this happy band set off for pony and trap ride round Queen's Park in 1955. One of the girls sports a corrective eye patch, a common sight at that time.

Glasgow was considered to be a dancing daft city in the heyday of the ballroom. The Dennistoun Palais, The Albert, The Plaza, Barrowland – everyone had their favourites. The chance to dress up and dance to the big bands was the highlight of the week. This is the Locarno in Sauchiehall Street in the late fifties.

In the pre-television age, parades and street fairs were big events from Lanark to Largs. In 1938 this hillbilly band was a big noise at Lanark's Lanimer fair, which is still going strong today.

Lanimer Day again, this time in 1959. This is not the famous Shotts and Dykehead Pipe Band but these bearded kilties were having just as much fun.

Below: After the pipers a touch of glamour. These Lanimer Day girls enjoyed dressing up as pirates and flower girls. Again in the fifties.

A dance round the Maypole before the main parade at the 1948 Lanimer Day.

Of the thousands who weekly pass through Glasgow airport for Florida or the Spanish costas, few are even aware that Renfrew was once home to the city's airport. But in the twenties and thirties the crowds flocked to air displays. In the foreground of this Renfrew shot is an autogiro, a forerunner of the helicopter which was largely forgotten until its reappearance in a Bond film.

Another popular form of home-grown entertainment, the highland games. The crowd sits under the 'hanging tree' to watch the piping contest at the 1930 Inveraray Highland games.

Right top: Race-going fashion in the 1930's. Hamilton Park is the setting as these gentlemen train their binoculars on the home straight.

Right bottom: A different kind of event but no less exciting. American harness racing at Scotstoun showground in 1978.

Golf is a popular Clydeside hobby and the area's many great courses have attracted the world's best. Turnberry is a particular favourite and a wonderful television advert for the glories of Scotland. A hallmark of the Scottish fan is good behaviour – though the millennium open at St. Andrews caused some concern. This is Turnberry in 1957 during a match-play championship and a huge gallery watches Scotland's legendary John Panton.

These tents are a far cry from the modern lightweight, high-fashion items of today. Holidays under canvas were a very popular way of getting away from the grime of the city. This is Lunderston Bay just south of Gourock in 1936.

A more regimented formation, as would be expected at this Officer Training Camp at Gailes near Irvine in 1938.

A picture that captures a day 'Doon the Watter' in the late sixties. Not an inch of space to spare on Barassie beach. The ever necessary windbreak is in use, family cars clog the sands, the ice cream van does a roaring trade and dad reads his newspaper.

Left: Typical beachwear for the mid fifties. Eighteen-month-old Kevin Thompson explores the beach at Rothesay, looking for a good place to start digging.

Left: A backcourt at Thistle Street, Gorbals, was the venue for this open air concert to raise money for old folk. The Kinning Park Ramblers, using a lorry as a stage, turn up the volume as hundreds of locals crowd into the spaces between washhouses and coal cellars while others resort to time-honoured windae-hingin'. The entertainment was a mixed bag of rock 'n' roll, highland dancing and comedy skits. Also on the bill, the Laurieston Pipe Band and one Alex Harvey who would find fame as leader of the Sensational Alex Harvey Band in the seventies.

Top: Quoits was once a very popular game, especially in Lanarkshire, and the odd serious wager was not unknown. This picture captures the essence of the game at the Scottish Championships in Larkhall, 1981.

Another winning shot as Kingston extend their 8-1 lead over Ayr Craigie in the 1979 Scottish Woman's Bowling Association championships at Rutherglen.

A serendipitous juxtaposition of two of Clydeside's great enthusiams – golf and shipbuilding. The tall cranes of the yards are a backdrop to competitors in the boys golf championships at Renfrew in the seventies.

Right: The river is not just for work! Rowing has a long and honourable tradition on Clydeside. Always an attraction for photographers, it could inspire memorable action shots like this.

Not quite Henley but this summer day on the banks of the Clyde at Glasgow Green produces a sylvan scene not normally associated with the heart of the Gorbals!

Left: The many bridges are a natural grandstand when there is action on the water. Here at Glasgow Green crews exercise under the watchful eye of strollers who have seen it all before. The powerful telescopic lens used provides an unusual view looking west in 1979.

Marathon running enjoyed a peak of popularity in the 1980s. Donald McGregor from Fife celebrates winning the 13th annual World Veteran Championship at Bellahouston in 1980.

Right: Meanwhile some way back up the course. . . . In fact this is the 1993 Glasgow Marathon and these two heroes dig deep to find the strength to carry them the last few gruelling miles to the finish.

Not the end of the road but the start. In the early days of the marathon the start was just south of Glasgow Cross and the hundreds of athletes thundered up High Street en masse. Yet another memorable image of life on Clydeside.